While I Was Dancing

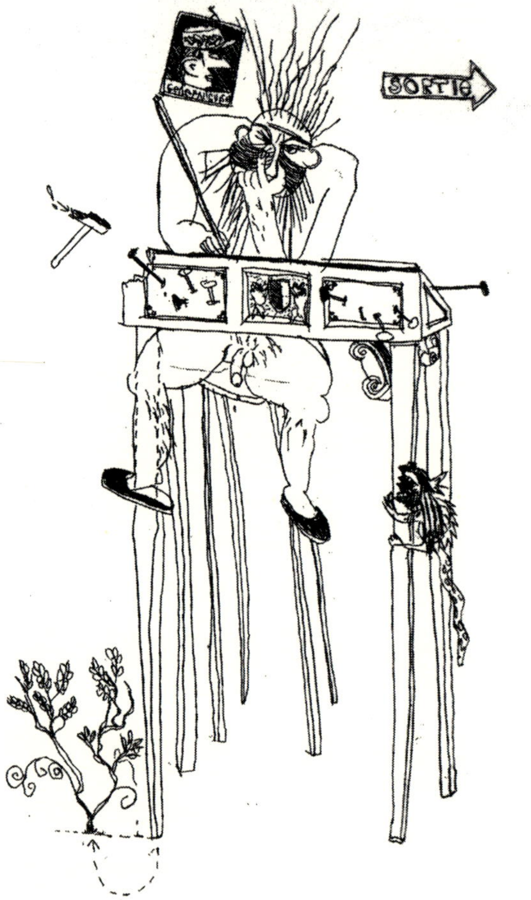

Ausgang / Exit

While I Was Dancing

22 Poems

BY STEVE CLORFEINE

With etchings by Christoph Zihlmann

CODHILL

CODHILL PRESS
New Paltz New York

Also by Steve Clorfeine

Beginning Again

In the Valley of The Gods

Field Road Sky

CODHILL PRESS

New Paltz New York

www.codhill.com

ISBN 1-930337-45-0

Cover art: Christoph Zihlmann

This book is dedicated to
The Naropa University and
the lineage of dancers and writers

Contents

Introduction

This collection of poems was written between 2004-2009. Working with various partners I developed a form, "moving and writing," in which one person moves with eyes closed and the other witnesses the movement, after which both write, "free writing" style. Then the other person moves and both write again.

Witnessed moving with eyes closed is based on a form called Authentic Movement, pioneered by Mary Starks Whitehouse and later, by Janet Adler. They brought to a generation of dancers, educators and therapists an improvised mindfulness-awareness practice, which Whitehouse called "movement in depth...moving and being moved."

I was first introduced to the practice while teaching at the School For New Dance in Amsterdam in 1991 and have since then had hundreds of duets with friends, colleagues, and students.

The medium of dancing/moving with eyes closed...what is revealed when the activity of imagining is primary, when the less visible or invisible becomes visible...the substance of shapes, sounds, images, stories that surface; how they mingle and compound; how they lead one deeper into the unknown and point to mysteries. And find their way back to the familiar and expressible.

I've felt this in the writing and monologues/stories of people I've worked with in this form over the years. Improvisation training encourages by-passing familiar mental processes and through non-linear, associative pathways, accessing another layer of memory, feeling, awareness. Again, making the invisible visible.

The "he" or "she" who shows up in most of these poems is my voice remembering the images and sensations of moving or witnessing my partner moving. And catching personal memories, events, phrases that come up alongside the witnessing and dancing.

ELEANOR'S DANCE

Eleanor, her merry stretch free licking
fingers spread in air
puffed blouse shoulders
toes flexed on
paint splattered wooden slats

Eleanor, lean sinew and
all smooth skin
(I am singing in the way I first knew)

Eleanor, suppose she can and
there you have it
everything is possible
(we become partners just like that)

Eleanor, we like what you're doing
we like the music
and look for ways to surround it
bring it forth

Victory to fingertips
(their willingness to fill the air).

IN THE FOYER

She smooths an Indian rug
(in circles with one hand)

explores the nap
the paisley flowers
the cream background her
closed eyes don't see

(the blue wall
the hovering prayer flags
the dropped ceiling
the frets and creaks

all what she doesn't see.)

She's smoothing in circles
finding her way upright.

She's swaddled in riotous colors
shawls wrapped and tied about
and stamping the floor
stamping the blue indoor
outdoor
runner
sprawled across the gray carpet.

Swaddled and stamping
and sprawled
her arms slice and
scythe
and hoe.

(small sounds that gutter the work she's doing
that promise a journey back
the place her grandparents cut hay
and dug potatoes).

She's determined now
she knows where to reach

yes

a daring grope in darkness
points the way.

Six small arm circles parallel the floor
uttering
sighing
languid
breathing
(almost done now).

WHO WILL LOOK AFTER HER WHEN THE CHILDREN ARE GONE?

her black velvet cape
the tall chair
pushed against the counter
olive pits in gray ceramic dish
unfinished solitaire game

(disquieting to find nothing more)

cupboards, freezer, as they were
she remembers the robin mother on her nest
outside the back door under the shed roof
and mind yourself going out there
she's been told

please God, her mother would say at some point
no more dreams,
no more
not of dead ones please

(even so tender their old voices
their wrinkled smiles)

outside the kitchen window
schoolkids on Wall Street this morning
small backpacks over hooded jackets
benevolent teachers and nuns

O Mary mother of God, they sing
the statue of the Virgin under morning shadows
in gloriam, in spring
red tulips falling on churchyard stones.

A JOURNAL OF POSITIVE FUTURES

Johanna climbs a narrow ladder
like steps into the sky
a white cap with brim flipped
covers the small curls of her hair
paintbrush in her back pocket

she will paint stars
the room will light up
we'll see the others
my wife (Johanna's older sister)
the two brothers, shirtless

they will talk about geography
Johanna will tell the story of the steps
while my wife plays the violin
and the two boys
shred newspapers
break sticks
fashion a hut, a fire pit

smoke will rise then
and the air fill with scents
of sizzling new potatoes

Johanna paints the last star
she descends the ladder
lies down on the ground near the hut
her three siblings surround her
their bodies and the small fire warming.

DWELLING

if he would excuse the demons
pay them off
suggest a holiday
for a few days.

alone in the house then
the other life
the no stumbling
the one that goes easily forth and back

the waking dreams
quiet
(not silenced
just resting).

now. will he surface and do a jig
have a shot of something?

reclaim both of him from hiding?
one cave, two of him.

a small dragon just waking
learning to live in human skin
to move together
to make sounds
to get familiar.

(a damn good thing)

a brief finale:
they herd themselves in the small space
like surf
like waves
they ride their single double
double single-ness

homely
yet compatible.

(and we?
we all swim ahead

who knows?
maybe the odds are in our favor).

HELP IS ON ITS WAY

a simple life watching baseball on TV
smoking cigarettes among kangaroo rats
in the desert

an unexpected e-mail from a young friend who writes
I'm a teen-age existentialist
and weeps on the page about
America destroying its youth

myself, a convict
padding around the morning
starting from scratch

okay lose everything
so what

only days later
I set out with her silver-handled suitcase
one side painted with a silver snake

Jeez, she writes on the postcard, *Jeez*
are you another stealth bomber
going up in smoke?

EPIFANEIA

she came in like that, my mom, after all it was her
favorite situation
mostly women various ages of course and she the
oldest and only dead one.

how dead?

the funny part is
she wants to look me in the eyes
(ancestral protection, from her side she can't resist)

you're the child who wants the truth
and I'm the mother who's reminding you
(so there)

reminder enough
my first dharma teacher asks
do you really want to be enlightened
not what I was expecting that last visit

today I'd say
alive a few times a week
(really alive
that's how close it gets)

I've got no answer.

she walks on stilts
she carries a bowl of fruit in her wedding crystal
punch bowl
the one that sits in the basement
next to where
leather-bound books decay
and debris litters the shelves

in the dream she's wearing striped socks
gray and black
perfectly young
perfectly ordinary
declaiming:

señores y señoras
bananas are not yet ripe
grapes are still suspended mid-air

I think of symbols
defer to the Greek linguist

epifaneia
appearing on the surface
phane, to appear

(like joining yourself to yourself
being visible).

"WE HAVE BURIED SO MUCH... THE DELICATE MAGIC OF LIFE"

after D.H. Lawrence, "Etruscan Cypresses"

Uncover as he would there was always more
the way he clenched his teeth
for example
the hairline he pretends not to notice
his running-on mind
extravagant nightmares
(*all inclusive*)

Her shoulder's curve
the dive in slow motion
crouching low
which sets the sirens going
and strikes the air

(keep 'em coming boys!)

Another time he made a hit
in skeleton costume
fingers furled
one protruding fang

(am I your personal sky protector?)

Tender she is
soft inside herself
startled when a voice barks

squat and rise, squat and rise
all passengers in Terminal One

He meanwhile (*whisper*)
meet me at the Playa Organza
molten sand
another search for identity

Hola señora
he would say
practicing casual reconnaissance
but no way

(hung out to dry again)

Back at the split level house
we find them like kissing fish
moving their mouths together
gliding through foliage
swooning on a slate patio

(repel the brand of holiday destinations)

She's next in sturdy corduroys
ones she can't replace
trivial yet meaningful to her

love that wraps her
fits her
gray side, black side
white side, back side, etc.

The way his mind goes

one moment
an omelet rising in the pan

next, an evening in the Himalayas
while snow peaks swallow the sun

After dessert
they wind their way through clipped lawns
file past gravestones
pronounce names dates of neighbors, forebears
internalize what's at hand

Who calls your name?

Her, yours? You, hers?

Finally, like crescendo or denouement
bursts a line spoken years before in a dream:

because I am heartbroken then you break my heart.

A DREAM APART
(for Susan Sontag)

1.

he's shaken wild in the night
awake, he identifies the sound
a small bomb
he distinguishes this from a missile
from a car blast, a direct hit
which it's not
no shouts or screams
this one just explodes, then quiet
lapsed long enough to doze again

2.

in the day
his body no longer jerks
at night, on the edge of sleep or dream
his heart recoils
a feeling which precedes the spasm in
his left shoulder
pulls his neck
the next day
offers up discomfort

3.

he notices when thoughts turn sideways
how certain memory twists his mind

under former circumstance
it would be welcome
help unwind the knots

by now it's daybreak
dogs come out of corners
daybreak and for the moment
he's forgotten the small bomb

neighborhood sounds renew
and everyone, friend or foe, is about to
or soon will
brew whatever boiled water onto fresh stems
adds to last night's still wet tea leaves.

4.

he's dressed in black
not intentional as much as
running out of warm clothes
no washing most weeks
save the lulls in fighting
when tap water runs longer

his clothes resemble the outfit he wore
even two weeks ago
the same pants
the sweater too warm then

his fingers more creased, more spotted
veins on back of hands more pronounced

he moves them now to warm them

what's increased is awareness, its edge
his lookout for danger spots
often now his mind runs this way.

5.

the first time was never the same again
he rolls across the fields what seemed like
mutual imagining, himself and Spring
the midlands yellow green
darkness after supper and darker
with dishes put away

strife then also
debate drew close in rooms
heated by, excited by, prospects

if the peace holds he thinks
the best of them will continue to be heard
will be understood
will win out.

6.

he's strong in his youth
he cries out to the hills
he cries out only to know who returns the call
even then
voices infatuate him

the old Jewess in the house beyond the stream
once she answered and
later he brought her a bag of coal
broke his fear of her
snapped it
which led to other shifts
cracks in the taut sphere of family

he wants everyone to answer his call
it's how he supposes you know things
impelled as he is by voice
needful as he is to be heard

later he thinks
had he directed his voice
turned it inside out in his body
the other, the needful
would not have grown so large.

7.

this would be the right moment
uncertainty then fierce benevolence
the shape and mood like laundry in courtyards
suspended, limp and stiff
or waving free, loosed in air

he entertains options
(another way to distract emptiness)
priming it, lubricating
he knows to coax it from sidelines
to absorb its nuance
he feels it, palpable, current
different from the daydream or the fear.

8.

the saviors he thinks
got it wrong
no, he got it wrong

most of them were really friends
or at least made no demands
it was up to him to resolve that no one
no one could do what he needed
himself to do

admiring them
imitating their light
it didn't work that way
this alone took years to reckon.

9.

his teacher wrote about fuzzy horns
and what happens
as the bone grows through the flesh and sharpens

he connects this to his wish
the physical urge to grow
(which in its absence
he recalls especially)

how he remembers it

presently

wind enters the arteries
four sides, six sides, eight sides
all sensation

and softness arrives

fullness

how simple just to stop
to find the moment

presently

like the small bomb
identified

sudden and whole.

NEWS FROM BASEMENTS

we eavesdrop on the world
on umpteenth remedial try
enter secretly
reach the underbelly
only to be pinned down
silenced again

slow
her face to
the sun
unmoving
waiting
weighing
wanting to
whisper and
no one is there

umbrellas in hand
pancaked widows
walk in pairs
paired their shadows
the dancing waiters
cakewalk on new year's day

hey there step up to the mike

look out for me
that millimeter edge of groove

at sunset I await your return
to be soft
to be at least
in a better mood

face up to sky
and return to normal
(still wanting)

help yourself to popcorn
make a dry martini

we are yearning
repeat, *we are yearning*
(in sign language)

and
(to myself)

bring back
bring it back

appearance

satisfaction

question

flicker

empty

fall away.

BY THIS MERIT

an early aviator:
wings on shoulder blades
hopeful a burst of wind will catch him
lift the slatted wings and
fly victorious

January of
gray apparel
please yourself
with shapely words
get a running start
(new year after all)

earthbound
we care so much
worry over greasy pans doors
that don't shut proper

the man sticks with his pipe and newspaper
where are you now?

the wife counts stitches
no longer hiding
knows tricks he'd not expect
content by the fire

each
their memory of first love
then the habits

who would fold the towels when
and if the soap drained down
where cotton or iodine
blades, the small scissors

early on
his mind creates
two of them
in cast iron claw foot bath

(and this is the point)
neither one concerned for outcome

that one moment
together in flesh in skin in water

later
he lights his pipe the fire the
first stitched row pleases her

they too a pair of slatted wings
hopeful for wind.

THE WAY HE KNOWS IS BY REFLECTION ON WATER

his gaze otherwise steady
inward
okay an occasional itch but
hey
flies don't really matter

the part of him that smells the other part
like a dog
senses alert

paddle in hand embarking
crossing descending like
sleep and waking
he asks himself
(even as a boy he asks)

is it enough any of it
to be rewarded/punished
do the games the pleasures
have secret meanings
are things pre-determined
can it be lost/forsaken?

take me across he hears
uncertain whose voice but sure, yes
he thinks of the bodhisattva, later
Shakyamuni
who offers his body to a starving tigress

that kind of taming, like Saraha
an arrowsmith in wild forests singing
dohas to the King, the Queen, the People

from his small chair in the corner of the room
overlooking the park
he reads to himself
(even before he knows the words he
remembers the story)

CALLED BACK

1.

In the beginning he's lifted
currents of air that enter like breezes
through sheer curtains.

In the middle he's overtaken by the scent of
his surroundings
the same with taste: he wants to lick the air and
go further.

Without comment he drinks it in and
patience replaces brooding.

Floral patterns, then moist red earth
umbrella of trees, darting insects
weeds, thickets, the whole span alive and moving.

In the end he stands unguarded
dispatched forward.

2.

On the occasion of a nautical event
(a regatta?)
he descends in an ocean of sensation
divides his time negotiating the watery
culture below the surface
and taking into account the metaphor of this.

Familiar images swim along
absorbed by slow strokes he remembers to
relax the divide
below and above.

Later, lifted by aspiration, loving direction
for how it invites articulate steps.

Like this, on earth, he inhabits his joints:
shoulders, hips, knees
lead the way.

At the same time he asks
what is the way?

His face invites moisture
he checks for constellations above
checks also the time his mind has flown.

3.

In a fortunate birth he comes back
the temples are always the same
the stones take their time
(not a bad thing to consider).

Again he loves beauty and this time
its inner way appears sooner.

He feels how shape both offers and records sensation
like moving along the seasons or making a dance.

Some days he feels shut inside
but even then he's called to natural events

spiders climbing, hanging mid-air
his feet stepping over rocks, knees bending

kneeling to observe, like his old friend in a dream
who crawls across South America noticing only the ground.

Light changes
dark enters in brushstrokes.

4.

He rejoices in a safe harbor
one arm held behind to ward off lingering doubt.

Smooth cobbles underfoot
the click his shoes have.

5.

Could it be the same woman cooking fish near
the town center?

The crowded square coming into view
conversations, distinct and local rhythm.

He weaves through 'til midday when all disperse
and he remains, waiting, hot sun on cobblestones.

6.

The same day, twilight in a hemlock grove
he throws grain in four directions
(a secret from a Freemason ancestor).

Owls, a roost of them woo him with nocturnes
their rayed feathers concealed by darkness

That night he climbs the high ridge
humming soft Yiddish tunes
all along the way.

The wordless songs arrive unbeckoned
and this he knows
will please all creatures of the mountain.

FORGETTING HOW REMEMBER WHEN

must have been afternoon, not winter
entrance bare of boots
pegs on wall bare of wool coats

Julius, the grandfather, wasn't trembling then
(Parkinson's still months away)

fixed ideas those years
family a given, solid
the boy has room to squirm
maneuver, not exit

the Doberman owned by the teenager Jimenez
(who doesn't even live there)
creates fear this first time, first big fear
(Sunday fear)
alone in playground

Jimenez he admires on the court short and fast
can hit a jump shot way outside the key
(the dog tied to the bench, snarling, pulling its leash)

the evergreen shrubs not yet chest high as
they will be later when he practices leaping over
to catch a long fly ball
now your knee can part the shrub still moving
and get through faster than a leap

minding gears in the elevator
alone, slowly, he comes upstairs
daydreams onto squares of linoleum
does he already have his own key?

they are sitting in the living room
the grandfather's brown suede jacket
the one he wore in the gray Nash
on the drive to California

the adults are talking so they don't notice
they are smoking and the smoke catches the
afternoon light

his child world muffled tears
the football's stunning impact
still taut and vibrating his right temple

he recognizes this as discontinuous
moments ago in the playground knocked flat
on concrete
(stands here more silent, lonely than that)

the grandfather looks up from
gold rim spectacles
tidy brown trousers against the green tweed slipcover
smooth with age, sunlit cheek

it's one last time the gaze is steady
one last before the years of trembling
speech foreshortened
hesitant slow dying

across the room the boy is touched
the grandfather's smile as if
they both know what's coming

smoke hangs in the sunlight
wordless testament
feelings they share this moment
love passes through, temporary we journey

grow old grow young
grow old grow young.

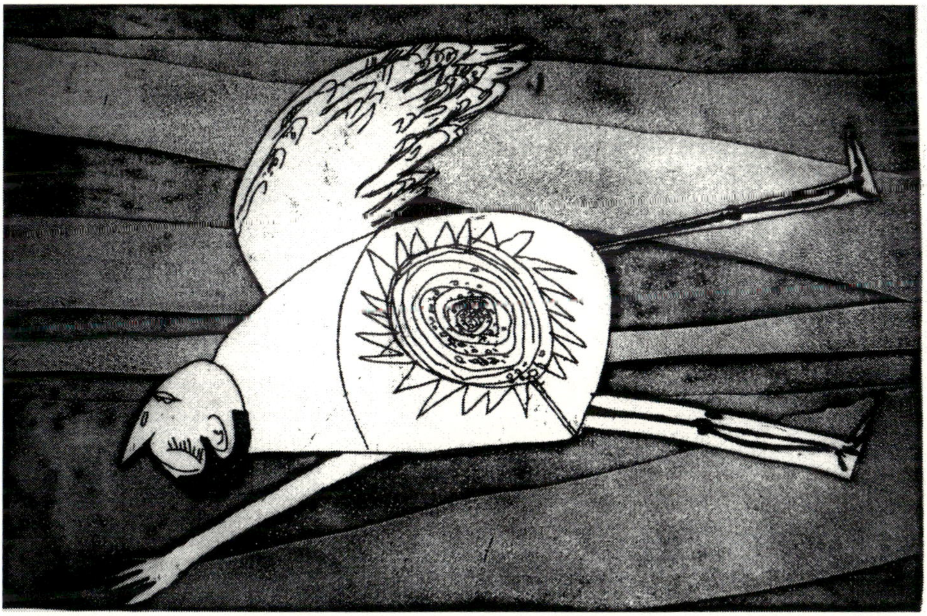

Mit einem dicken Bauch kann man nicht gut fliegen / Difficult to Fly With a Big Belly

Etchings by Christoph Zihlmann

Gefangen / Imprisoned

Zacken von oben, Zacken von unten / Jags From Above, Jags from Below

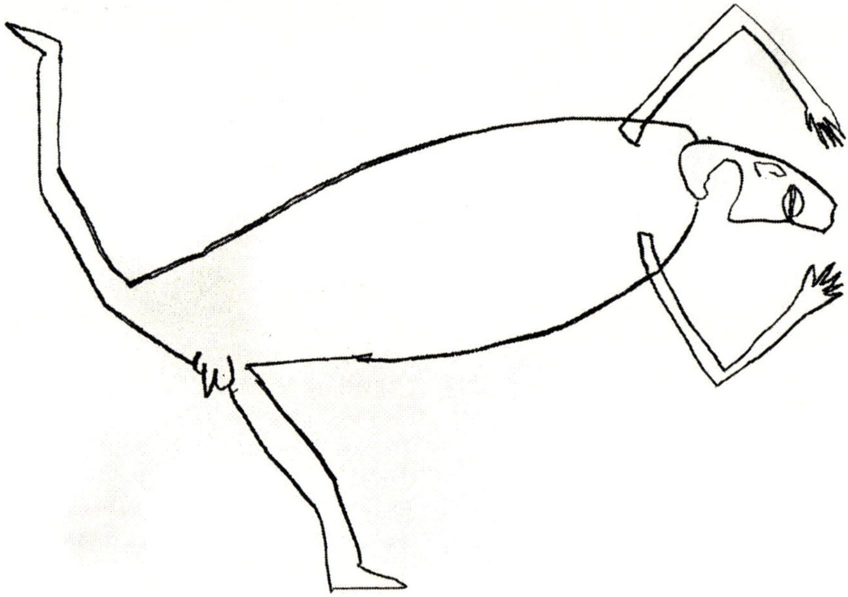

Läufer (Laeufer) / Runner

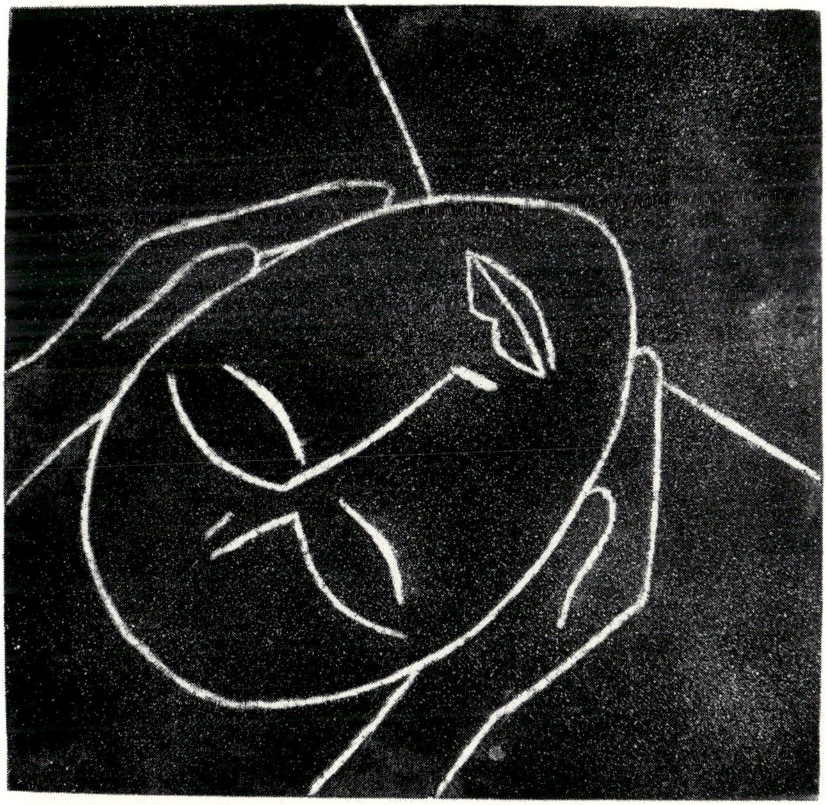

Es ist gut so / It's OK

ON WINGS

Remembering comes on wings
the school auditorium wooden seats
rows connected
labeled
metal numbers
letters
fitted with tiny screws

please rise for the national anthem
right palm pressed to left breast

the teacher
Angela DeSantis
Miss DeSantis
(gray hair firmly parted)
reads us stories of
queens and princes
(we think she knows how it works)

he was the prince one time
(and that despite life-threatening reprimands
about carrying the goldfish bowl)

Santiago his friend
doe-eyed dullard
sweet like processed jellies we get
in the lunchroom
(peel back the top of the small plastic tub)

let me fly
Santiago says
darting side to side
feeling his arches
(his feet hold such secrets)

taking off
without destination
or landing strip

(winging it like we both want)

flying we know as
well-being
thoughts erased

on until dusk
until shadows rule
and close the glory.

ANGELS

1.

Inside this beam of recognition
(odds on the lighted way)

where slipshod drifts off
and he dances with remainders

moves with accuracy
staccato here curves there

he outlasts sentiment and
ends up redeemed
like the bottom of compost filtered
    into warm soil

2.

In parks he notices pigeons
familiar urban uniform
gray-blue, blue-black
occasional white-brown

in fields other birds
mid-spring the red-winged blackbird
bluebirds in pairs
orchard orioles late spring
around corn planting

(a beginner in naming them he starts late
misses the rose-breasted grosbeak startled
    on the road the instant flight upward)

3.

Like angels
one in second grade
lifts him high above the classroom
(the first of many visits)

unspoken for decades until someone says
angels never go far

and he remembers flying with Santiago the
    dark boy
whose place in the classroom
is a single desk near the closet

4.

He becomes the master of tiny things
and remembers:

spiral shapes in sand happily washed away
blue saw grass in wild southern fields
cricket songs on summer nights

arguments in the clouds
applause from the underworld

(before hours are counted
before the beasts are born)

MONICA VITTI

1.

He moves and speaks
in small chops
(more Gogo than Didi)

it's his nature to be puzzled
to speak wide and high without signs
for the uninitiated
(even she, he worries, might not know)

sometimes he favors silence
sometimes just locked down

when a child enters he forgets and
how and where he really wants to be
re-enters
irresistible.

2.

Stray moonlight
awake and rambling
recalling this in middle night
a cup of tea
silent house

3.

He recalls long steps to Italian museums
deft hand gestures
and in Firenze too much memory
(not his alone)

Bologna dark with simple restaurants
in Rome expecting
Monica Vitti
blond and roomy eyed
her slightly crushed nose
(who could resist)

the way she leans on Mediterranean air
(it's Antonioni's *L'Avventura)*
not sure if she wants to be swallowed or not

4.

Of the many he meets, one says of all places
    she's traveled
the one she hates is Venice

5.

In all these cities
he plays a detective
a dark mysterious outlaw
a hit man for a dictator

roles he's been assigned despite
his gentle nature
(so he thinks)

anonymous in these evils
counting applause or jeers
(though who knows how Italians understand)

still, he is certain of translation
certain of himself.

how else to walk onstage?

ELSEWHERE

Oh he says
stutters
and despite himself
enters the episodic uncertainty of speech

Oh Oh Oh
like *Uh-Oh*
a crossword clue
two words two letters.

He dives with elephant trunk
stands on toes
twirls hands like mechanical street sweeper
    brushes.

Defiant
ever angry at same things
involuntary rudeness
regression like tidal wave.

Oh Oh Oh
this time a groan
deeply resist
yet again upright

(sternum like warrior like smooth sail).

Nobody requests a plebiscite
we change context and relax
human again, well disposed
the world expands its natural
    way

Sheer wind
we kites rip tide against clouds
like young ones tumble
    downhill

like cut grass
random
parades its fertile scent.

ACCORD, ECUADOR

Syllables stretch
reach back to
lingua franca
where all voices accord
chorus of prayer or
celebration

creatures in the vicinity
(doves peck stray seeds)
wild onions, mustard grass
lambs quarters so
moist and fresh
we don't hesitate to eat the dirt

this is no time to make decisions she says
at the end of a long conversation
leave the interrogation 'til after the lilacs
'til first of peony buds

(has she heard the red haired heroine in the
    background?
has she seen the child disguised with mustache?)

he senses himself closing in
cutting back on rambling if only
he could remember

what remarks
what constitutes evidence

(there is nothing abrasive
there is only forgetting)

grow robust again

her face against blossoms
Bradford pear
distant wild cherry

ladder downwind
against one sugar maple

continents arise in schoolboy shapes
fit together in ways they won't ever

geography is imagination

the impact is stunning

move from Accord
deposit South America for example
take Peru and dive into Ecuador

CRACOW

Question:
is the damp arena of my mind fertile or corrosive?

(she writes this from her duplex inside the old
    family house
off a tram route in the northern part of the city)

she's well trusted
an older woman who lives
in the original family house
split down the middle
mother and sister
on the other side of the wall

she's a musician, deep in thought
what about will, she asks
where does it come from?

SUSPEND

In cocoon of half sleep
the tickle of pages turning
tires on wet streets
strident horns

can we meet again
over scotch, coffee
make beauty out of nothing
over time
and time again

light slant rain

fogged in woods

liquid quiet of well-being

we fall off the horse and prepare to walk long distances

shy of apology

free of household dues

snare none in the net you cast

let them dissolve in salt air
in good sleep

(change the décor of disorderly minds)

BIRDS DREAM

1.

The bird and I fight naked
it throttles
I throttle
the sun bears down

when the bird's claws go rubbery on my flesh
that's how I know we're done

we are both crumpled, panting, listing
tangles of hair and feathers

I glance at the bird
who has the look of a child
returning from tantrums

(I've forgotten why we fight so fiercely)

2.

There will be no rain of doves
we will bite each other's noses
spit eye level

(no reign of doves)

gestures of improvement
will ruin us

how we face each other
how we face ourselves
begin again

OLD ONES

Old one
the one who keeps watch

the wrinkled one with heavy lids
yellow teeth what's left of them

bare sunken feet
crumpled toes

tunic and pants like
old laundry
left on a fence

wilted lips in fields of rye

What the old ones do:

Betty's mother records her solitaire games
on scratch pads
ten year's worth

old Ned lumbers about
his love for the woman upstairs
propels him to new heights at ninety-two
neither one of them hears a thing

Marko's father in Croatia
his rowboat motor rigged to
patient island dock
the outhouse collapsed and
rotted grapes he no longer presses

Harriet on her motorized golf cart
on the light machine
that allows her to see
words on a page
to fit the meaning together
her voice still sharp and full of herself
eats pastrami on rye before the bridge game

dementia-like Carla
who cries for grandma
for her dolls
speaks lost languages while
both daughters despair and change her gown

Great aunt Tanya
doctor I am not a number I am a human being
my name is Tanya

leads the chorus for
fellow octogenarians

most mornings tells herself
Tanya get up! Get out of bed! Do something!

dreams of the baby left behind
St. Petersburg, 1920
goes off as secretary to a White Russian
army captain
(lovers no doubt)
later the wrong side
but now
temporary protection
food and cigarettes

he dreams of Naomi in a royal blue
    satin dress
white cashmere sweater
she's working a bar
no longer an actress and finally happy

he dreams of Winnie who sits on his lap
    and tells everyone
how at nineteen he was already didactic

he riffs on questions in an interview
on a small town radio station
callers keep asking
and he is flawless
makes laughter
can't miss a beat
every line has something

before sleep he reads from the Hassidim:

keep two pieces of paper in your pockets at all times
on one write
'I am a speck of dust.'

on the other
'the world was created for me.'

Acknowledgments

The book cover and accompanying etchings are from the Swiss artist and architect, my dear friend Christoph Zihlmann.

Thanks to my dancing/writing partners over the years: Jenny Bates, David Daub, Jonathan Fox, Arawana Hayashi, Dennis McCarthy, Julie Rose, David Santner, and Sarah Stackhouse.

Remembering friends & relations whose images come up in these poems:

David Appelbaum, Alan Bates, Mark Bates, Kai Beavers, Brenda Bufalino, Jay Clayton, Myrtle Clorfeine, Lucy Dodd, Leslie English, Jerry Granelli, Susan Grossman, Lanny Harrison, Ivo Jozovic, Esther Katz, Elisabeth Merkli, Meredith Monk, Tanya Nitzburg, Betty Oliver, Susan Rethorst, Julie Tyler, Anne Waldman, Denie Whalen, Leland Williams.

Artist's Statement

I enjoyed painting and drawing since my childhood and youth; painting and drawing became a familiar and secure way of expressing myself.

I also have been fascinated by other aspects of visual art: one is that artwork is a means to accessing and contacting deeper areas of personality that usually are not accessible to the conscious mind; the immense richness and wisdom of this underground stream of life can be joined with the practice of art. Often I myself felt surprised by the outcome of this practice.

Another aspect that always intrigued me is that in a good realistic artwork some lines or color fields are able to create an absolutely vivid image of a person, an object, a situation in the mind of the viewer. I have been interested in exploring how this works and what is needed to create this vivid impression.

In the mid 1980's I had the opportunity to spend some time in the Centre Genevois de Gravure Contemporaine in Geneva, Switzerland, a studio for contemporary printing techniques. Besides having space and time for practicing art I had the chance to experience making art in a professional way and to get familiar with the techniques of etching. Working on the etchings was an inner and very personal process.

One body of work was a series of 20 etchings. These images came up from deeper places in my mind to consciousness as fully formed images. They had just to be brought to paper. They showed up with some energy and urgency and claimed to be acknowledged and seen. The series was not planned as such, rather the images came up one after the other and at some point the process was over, there was a relief, the last piece is an image of birth.

Another part of work was a smaller series of 7 etchings and some odd pieces. Working on the pieces of the small series always began with the image of a man sitting at a table, being serious, studying, thinking about things. The situation and incidents around the man and the table showed up while working on the plates. These pieces can be seen as improvisations or instant compositions.

I always had and still have controversial feelings about some pieces. The images of being hurt and imprisoned are somehow honest and true, but I see also a strong self-consciousness and a longing to be seen and acknowledged in them.

In this sense the process of working on the etchings was also one of getting in contact with this rich mixture of motivations for being an artist and working as an artist: exploration of self and of being a human; self- expression, but also self-consciousness, arrogance, desire to be recognized... so this process brought up aspects of the practice of art that I find were crucial for me to be confronted with.

Christoph Zihlmann,
Zurich, January 2010

Photo by Liane Stephan

Steve Clorfeine is a writer, performer, and facilitator with a long association to The Naropa University in Boulder, Colorado and the State University of New York at New Paltz. As an independent workshop leader, he presents training programs for theater teachers, actors, business leaders and at meditation centers throughout North America, Europe and Asia. Steve has collaborative relationships with many colleagues from arts disciplines including long standing partnerships with actress Lanny Harrison and musician Steve Gorn. In 2008–'09, he was awarded Cultural Envoy grants from the U.S. to create theater pieces in India and in Nepal. He has been a student of Shambhala Buddhist teachings since 1974. Steve lives with his wife in Kingston, New York and in New York City.

www.steveclorfeine.com